Planets in Our Solar System

EARTH

by Jody S. Rake

raintree
a Capstone company — publishers for children

Raintree is an imprint of Capstone Global Library Limited, a company incorporated in England and Wales having its registered office at 264 Banbury Road, Oxford, OX2 7DY – Registered company number: 6695582

www.raintree.co.uk
myorders@raintree.co.uk

Text © Capstone Global Library Limited 2021
The moral rights of the proprietor have been asserted.

All rights reserved. No part of this publication may be reproduced in any form or by any means (including photocopying or storing it in any medium by electronic means and whether or not transiently or incidentally to some other use of this publication) without the written permission of the copyright owner, except in accordance with the provisions of the Copyright, Designs and Patents Act 1988 or under the terms of a licence issued by the Copyright Licensing Agency, 5th Floor, Shackleton House, 4 Battle Bridge Lane, London SE1 2HX (www.cla.co.uk). Applications for the copyright owner's written permission should be addressed to the publisher.

Edited by Alison Deering
Designed by Jennifer Bergstrom
Original illustrations © Capstone Global Library Limited 2021
Picture research by Tracy Cummins
Production by Tori Abraham
Originated by Capstone Global Library Ltd

978 1 3982 0515 4 (hardback)
978 1 3982 0516 1 (paperback)

British Library Cataloguing in Publication Data
A full catalogue record for this book is available from the British Library.

Acknowledgements
We would like to thank the following for permission to reproduce photographs:
NASA: JSC, 21; Shutterstock: BlueRingMedia, 15, Brigitte Pica2, 27, buradaki, Back Cover, Claudio Divizia, 20, Daniel Prudek, 24, Denis Tabler, Cover, Diego Barucco, 18, Digital Images Studio, 19, Dotted Yeti, Cover Left, Good_Stock, 17, GraphicsRF, 26, ixpert, 1, kavram, 4, Kokhanchikov, 13, mapichai, 14, Marcos_Silva, 11, metamorworks, 6, Michael Rosskothen, 22, Nepster, 7, Oliver Denker, 25, Paopano, 23, PopTika, 9, Ronnie Chua, 28, S. Rickenbacher, 16, studio23, 10, Triff, 5, udaix, 12. **Design elements:** Shutterstock: Arcady, BLACKDAY, ebes, LynxVector, phipatbig, Stefan Holm, veronchick_84

Every effort has been made to contact copyright holders of material reproduced in this book. Any omissions will be rectified in subsequent printings if notice is given to the publisher.

All the internet addresses (URLs) given in this book were valid at the time of going to press. However, due to the dynamic nature of the internet, some addresses may have changed, or sites may have changed or ceased to exist since publication. While the author and publisher regret any inconvenience this may cause readers, no responsibility for any such changes can be accepted by either the author or the publisher.

Printed and bound in India

Contents

The blue planet 4

The air up there 10

Third rock from the Sun 14

Earth's Moon 18

Exploring Earth 22

Our planet, our home 26

    Fast facts 29

    Glossary 30

    Find out more 31

    Index 32

Words in **bold** are in the glossary.

The blue planet

Deep oceans and tall mountains cover its surface. Ice freezes and lava flows. Dry deserts and wet forests are homes for living things. Trees, flowers, fish and birds live here. A planet booms with life. This is Earth. This is our home.

Earth is full of life.

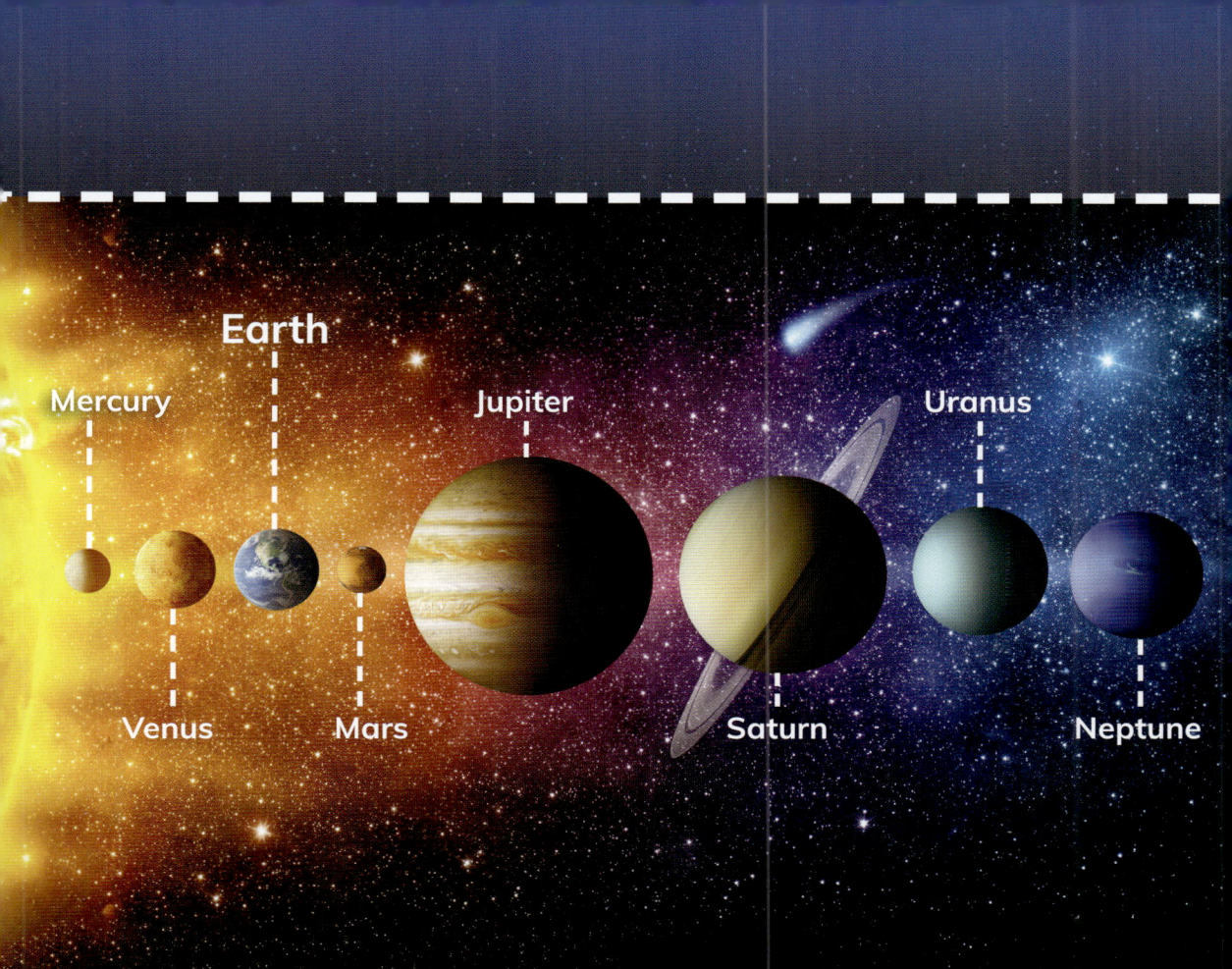

The planets in our solar system

Earth is the third planet from the Sun. It is the only planet in our **solar system** that has life.

Earth is the fifth largest planet. It is the largest of the rocky planets. There is an invisible line around the middle of Earth. This is called the **equator**. If you could drive around it in a car, it would take about 16 days.

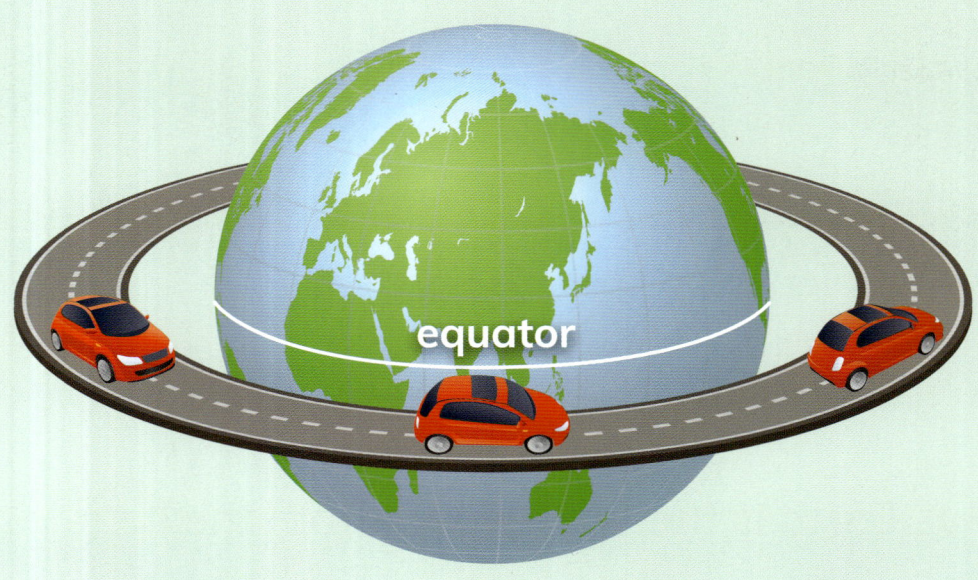

The equator circles Earth.

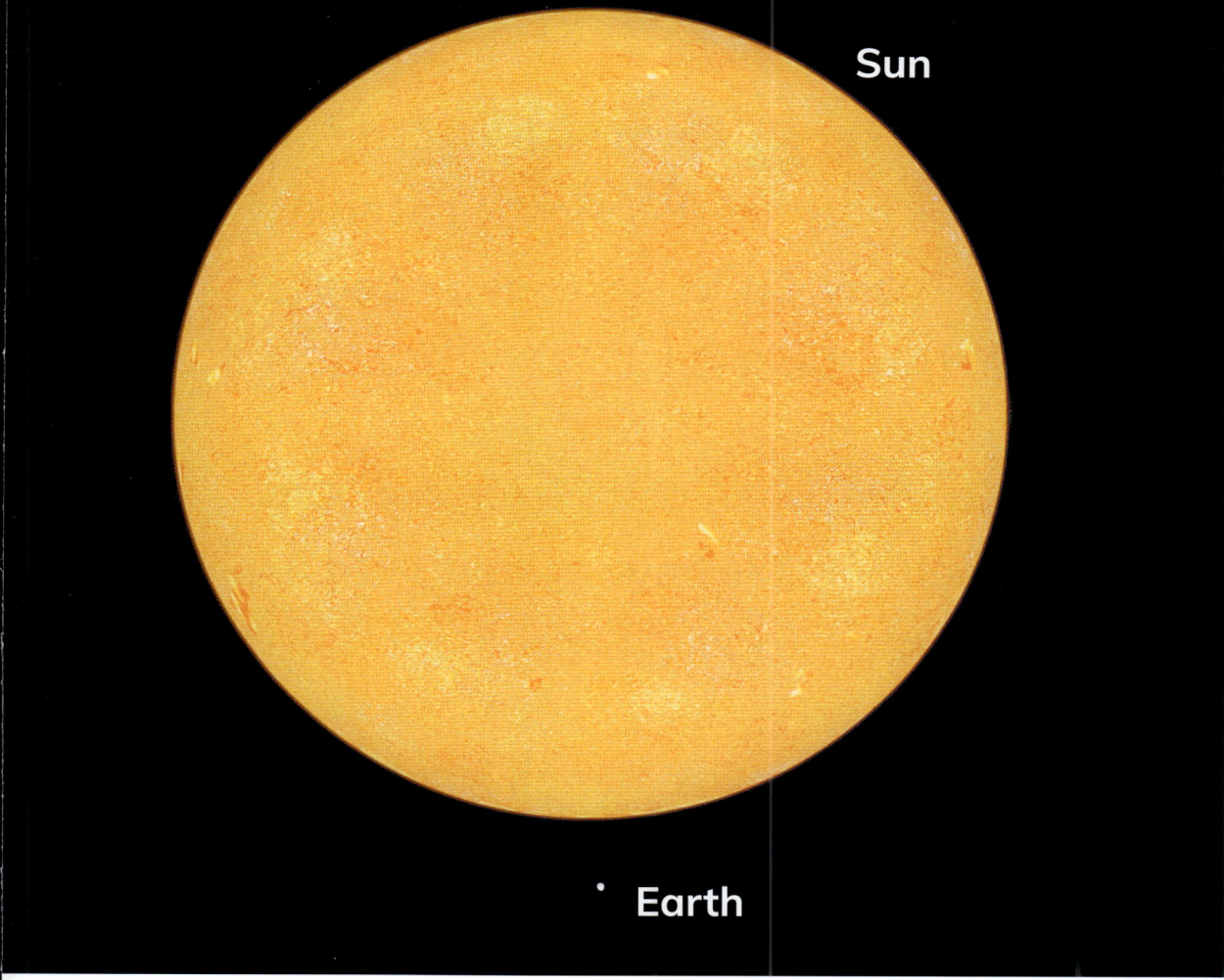

The Sun is much larger than Earth.

Earth is much smaller than the Sun. More than one million Earths could fit inside the Sun!

From space, Earth looks mostly blue. That is because it is mostly covered with water. Earth is sometimes called the "blue planet".

Earth was not discovered like other planets. People have always lived only on Earth.

Our planet was named long ago. *Earth* means "ground" or "soil". It is the only planet not named after a god or goddess.

Earth is often called "the world".

Earth, as seen from space

The air up there

Earth is millions of kilometres away from the Sun. It gets just the right amount of light and heat from the Sun.

There is a layer of gases around the planet. This is called the **atmosphere**. It is made of **oxygen** and other gases. These are important for life on Earth.

A layer of gases surrounds Earth.

The atmosphere protects the planet.

This layer also protects Earth. It protects us from the Sun. It holds in enough heat to keep us from freezing at night. It even protects Earth from space rocks called **meteors**.

Earth's atmosphere makes the sky look blue. How? Light from the Sun looks white. But it is really all colours. Light bounces off tiny specks of air and water. The way it bounces around gives things their colours.

How can we see blue colour?

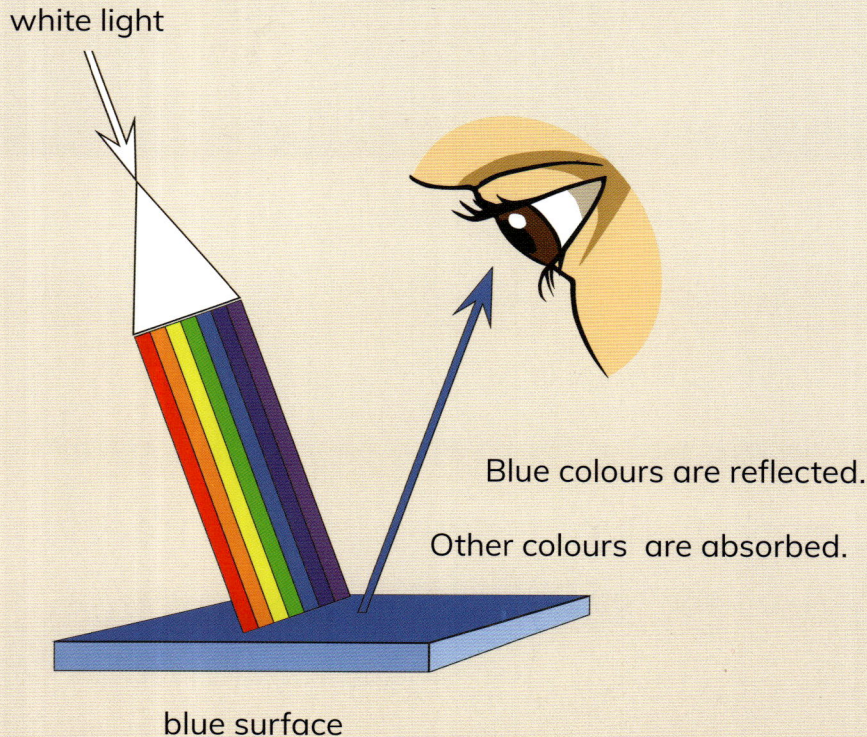

white light

Blue colours are reflected.
Other colours are absorbed.

blue surface

The sky looks blue on a sunny day.

Blue light bounces around the most. That's what we see when we look at the sky on a sunny day.

Third rock from the Sun

Earth moves around the Sun. It circles the Sun once every 365 days. The path Earth follows is called an **orbit**. It is not a perfect circle. It is shaped like an egg.

Earth also **rotates** (spins). It does this once every 24 hours.

Earth's orbit is not a perfect circle.

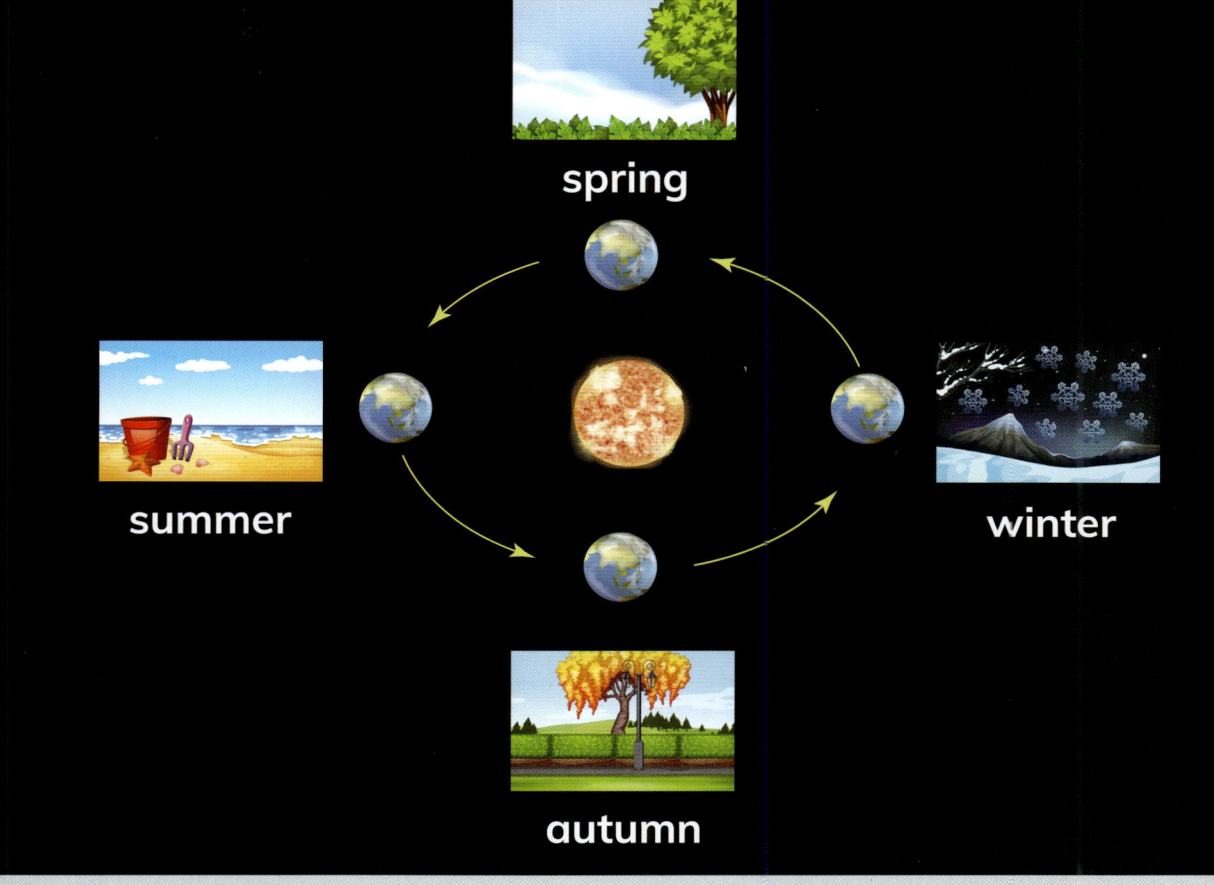

The way Earth tilts creates seasons.

Our planet is tilted slightly. That is why we have seasons. When the top half of Earth is tilted towards the Sun, it is summer there. When it is pointing away, it is winter. The seasons are opposite for the bottom half of Earth.

Earth is the only planet with liquid water.

Earth is a rocky planet. It is made of rock and metals. It was shaped by earthquakes, volcanoes and weather. These formed Earth's mountains and valleys.

Earth is covered with water. It is the only planet we know with liquid water. Oceans, lakes and rivers make up 70 per cent of the surface.

Earth has a **water cycle**. Water changes from a liquid to a gas. The gas rises. Then it turns back into water droplets. They form clouds.

The clouds let go of water when it rains. Rain falls on land. It is collected in bodies of water.

Earth's water cycle

Earth's Moon

Earth has one moon. It is far away. About 30 Earths could fit between us and the Moon. The Moon is about a quarter of the size of our planet.

Earth

Moon

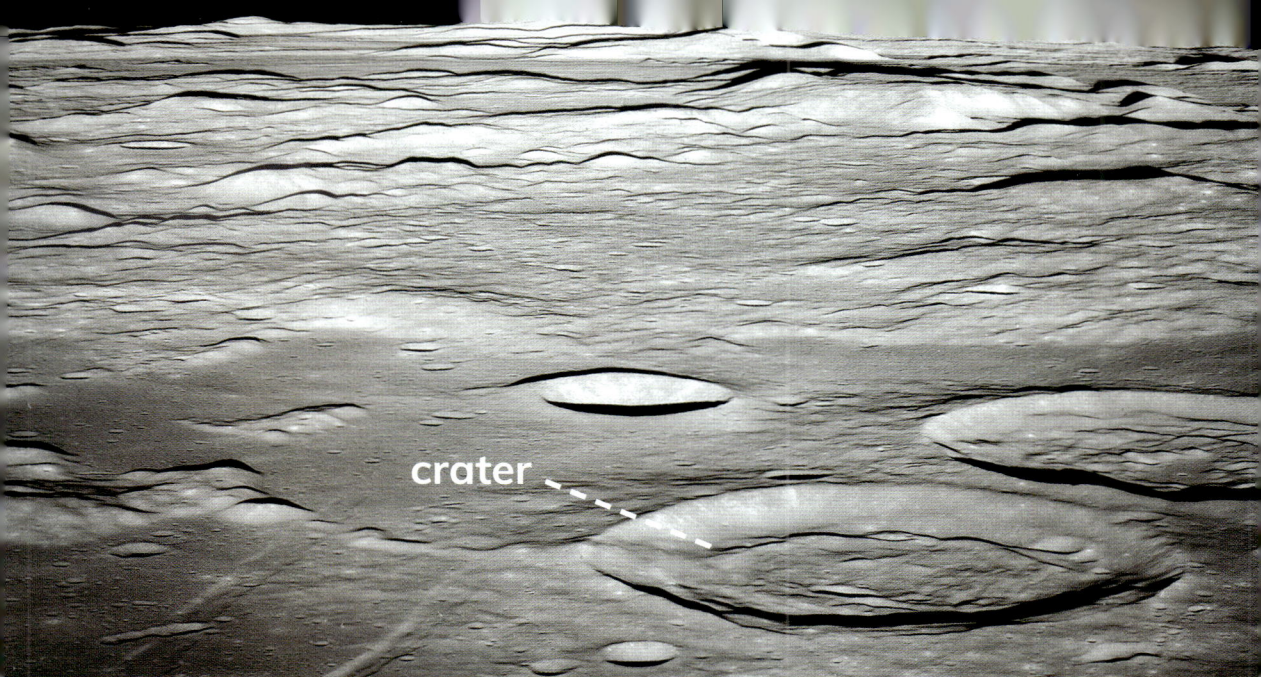

crater

The Moon is covered with craters.

The Moon is made of rock, much like Earth. Its surface is covered with fine grey dust. It is also covered with holes. These are called **craters**.

The Moon circles Earth once every 27 days. It also spins. It spins at the same speed as Earth. That is why we always see the same side of the Moon.

The Moon looks bright white in the night sky. This is because of light from the Sun.

Sometimes the whole of the Moon appears lit up by the Sun. This is called a full moon. Sometimes we see only part of the Moon. Then it looks like a half moon or **crescent** moon.

A man on the Moon

Many spacecraft have gone to the Moon. Some have only circled it. Others have landed. Only 12 people have ever been on the Moon.

Exploring Earth

People have been exploring Earth for thousands of years. We didn't always know how big our planet was. People built big ships to sail across the ocean. They found more land.

Ships explored our planet long ago.

A satellite circles Earth.

We built **satellites** to circle Earth from space. The first one took off more than 60 years ago. It sent information back using a radio.

Since then, many satellites have been launched. Today, almost 5,000 of them zoom around Earth!

Mount Everest is the highest place on Earth.

People have explored all over Earth. They have climbed mountains and hiked through jungles. The world's deep oceans are still being explored. More people have been into space than to the bottom of the ocean!

Earth's highest point is Mount Everest. It is high above sea level. The deepest part of the ocean is the Mariana Trench. It is in the Pacific Ocean. It is almost 11 kilometres (7 miles) deep.

The Mariana Trench is the deepest place on Earth.

Our planet, our home

Usually one year on Earth is 365 days. But really, it takes Earth a bit longer than that to circle the Sun.

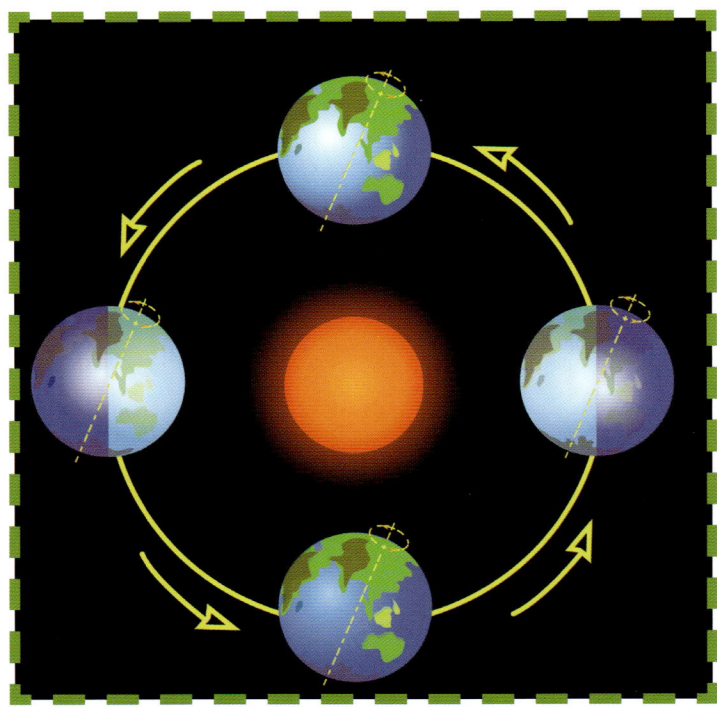

Earth orbits the Sun.

A leap year gives us an extra day.

Because of this, we have an extra day once every four years. The year with an extra day is called a "**leap year**". The extra day is added to the month of February.

Earth is the only planet we know that supports life. It is the perfect distance from the Sun. It has plenty of water.

Earth is home to more than 8 million types of living things, including us!

Earth is home to millions of living things.

Fast facts

Name:
Earth

Location:
third planet from the Sun

Planet type:
rocky

Moons:
1

Glossary

atmosphere layer of gases that surrounds some planets, dwarf planets and moons

crater hole in the ground made when large pieces of rock crash into a planet or moon's surface

crescent curved shape

equator imaginary line around the middle of Earth

leap year year of 366 days with 29 February as the extra day

meteor chunk of metal or rock that falls from space

orbit path an object follows while circling another object in space

oxygen colourless gas that people breathe; humans and animals need oxygen to live

rotate move or turn in a circle

satellite spacecraft that circles Earth; satellites gather and send information back to Earth

solar system the Sun and the objects that move around it

water cycle how water changes as it moves between the ground and the air

Find out more

Books

The *Inner Planets* (Super Space Science), David Hawksett (Raintree, 2019)

Solar System (DKfindout!), Sarah Cruddas (DK Children, 2016)

The Sun and Our Solar System (Great Scientific Theories), Jen Green (Raintree, 2017)

Websites

www.bbc.co.uk/bitesize/topics/zdrrd2p/articles/ztsdj6f
Learn more about the rocky planets.

www.dkfindout.com/uk/space
Find out more about space, including all the planets in our solar system.

www.esa.int/kids/en/home
Learn more about space exploration from the European Space Agency.

Index

atmosphere 10–12

blue planet 8

colours 12–13, 20
craters 19

days 14, 26–27
distance 10, 18, 28

equator 6

gases 10–11, 17

leap years 27
life 4–5, 10, 28
light 12–13

Mariana Trench 25
meteors 11
Moon 18–21
mountains 4, 16, 24–25
Mount Everest 25

name 8

oceans 4, 16, 22, 24–25
orbit 14–15, 19, 26

rocky 6, 16, 19

satellites 23
seasons 15
size 6–7, 18
solar system 5
spacecraft 21
Sun 5, 7, 10–13, 14–15, 20, 28

temperature 10–11

water 4, 8, 12, 16–17, 22, 28
water cycle 17

years 26–27